Information Technology Dictionary

Information Technology Dictionary

Gaynor Attwood
Lecturer, Department of Education, Bristol Polytechnic

Ian Attwood
Computer Room Manager, Rolls-Royce, Bristol

McGRAW-HILL BOOK COMPANY

London · New York · St Louis · San Francisco Auckland · Bogotá· Guatemala · Hamburg · Lisbon Madrid · Mexico · Montreal · New Delhi · Panama Paris · San Juan · São Paulo · Singapore · Sydney Tokyo · Toronto

Published by
McGRAW-HILL Book Company (UK) Limited
MAIDENHEAD · BERKSHIRE · ENGLAND

British Library Cataloguing in Publication Data
Attwood, Gaynor, *1948* –
Information technology dictionary.
1. Information systems – Encyclopaedias
I. Title II. Attwood, Ian, *1948* –
001.5

ISBN 0-07-707149-2

Library of Congress Cataloging-in-Publication Data
Attwood, Gaynor, *1948* –
Information technology dictionary / Gaynor Attwood, Ian Attwood.
p. cm.
ISBN 0-07-707149-2: £4.25
1. Electronic data processing – Dictionaries. 2. Information technology – Dictionaries. I. Attwood, Ian, *1948* – . II. Title.
QA76.15.A87 1989
004'.03 – dc20 89-12458
CIP

1 2 3 4 5 DP 8 9 1 0 9

Typeset by Hybert · Design & Type, Maidenhead, Berkshire and
printed and bound in Great Britain by Dotesios Printers Ltd, Trowbridge, Wiltshire.

To David and James

A

AI	artificial intelligence
ALU	arithmetic and logic unit
ASCII	American Standard Code for Information Interchange

access A term used to describe the action of obtaining information from a computer either from the central processing unit or from backing store. To access information means to retrieve information from a computer.

access time This refers to the time taken to get information from the computer's memory. It represents the time between issuing the command to get the information and the time at which the information is retrieved from the system for use. The information may be either in the computer's main memory or in secondary storage such as a disk.

acoustic coupler A type of modem that allows data to be transmitted over telephone lines without making an 'electrical' connection to the line. (See **Figure 1** on page 47.)

acoustic hood A printer cover or hood to reduce the noise; it could be considered as a lid to a printer.

acronym A group of letters formed from the first letters of other words, eg BASIC which is an acronym for **B**eginners' **A**ll-purpose **S**ymbolic **I**nstruction **C**ode.

Ada A high-level programming language often used for real time applications. It is named after Ada, Countess Lovelace.

address (1) A computer uses an address to locate information in its memory in the same way that you can be found at your address. Each location in the computer's memory will store a different piece of information.

address (2) An address can be used to identify uniquely devices that are attached to a computer, eg there will be a disk drive address.

alphabetic This describes any set of characters made up from the letters A to Z. It is a way in which data can be represented when stored in a data base.

alphanumeric This describes any set of characters made up of letters from A to Z and numbers 0 to 9. It is a way in which data can be represented when stored in a data base.

analogue information A measurement or representation of a quantity that can have any value between a lower and upper limit. The reading can be variable unlike a digital reading which is either on or off, or, at one value or another. (See **Figure 5** on page 51.)

analogue signal Information represented by a varying electrical voltage so that it can have any value between a lower and upper limit. It may be necessary to convert this signal into a digital form as the data sent by the computer to peripherals is often in the form of analogue signals whereas the computer will use digital signals.

application programs A description applied to programs that are written to operate on a computer so that you can perform a particular task. Examples include word processing, spreadsheets and desk-top publishing programs. (Compare and contrast with **utility program**.)

archived files This term refers to computer data files that are not currently being used by the system and which are stored away from it. These files may be at a remote site or in a fireproof safe.

arithmetic and logic unit (ALU) The part of the central processing unit that performs all the arithmetic and logic operations. For example, when a program adds two numbers or compares values in a data base, it is this part of the computer that provides the brain power.

array A structure containing one or more subdivisions each of which may contain data.

artificial intelligence (AI) An area of much research at the present time. It is concerned with putting computers to uses which involve the computer performing tasks as humans do, such as learning from experience and reasoning.

ASCII American **S**tandard **C**ode for **I**nformation **I**nterchange (pronounced ASK-KEY). A code used to represent upper- and lower-case letters, numbers and special characters.

The code uses 7 bits of an 8-bit byte to represent the character; this pattern allows for 128 possible combinations. It covers the 26 lower-case letters, 26 upper-case letters and ten numbers (0 to 9). The remaining bit is a parity bit which is used as a check on the correctness of the data. Examples of ASCII codes are A = 65 a = 97. (See **Figure 5** on page 51.)

assembly language A low-level computer programming language that is characterised by being specific to a machine type and is not transferable. Generally, one assembly language instruction translates into one machine code instruction.

authoring languages A collective term for programming languages that allow computer users to create learning and training materials without any detailed knowledge of programming.

autoboot A short computer program that will allow a program to be loaded or 'booted' automatically.

auto-repeat A term used to describe the repeating of characters on a screen or monitor by pressing the appropriate key continually.

B

BASIC	Beginner's All-purpose Symbolic Instruction Code

backing store A term used to describe memory storage outside the computer. It provides a 'back-up' to the computer's main memory. The main advantage is that it is possible to hold more information which can be called back when required. Backing store memory is non-volatile so that it is not lost when the computer is switched off.

Examples of backing store include floppy disk, hard disk and magnetic tape.

Backing store is also referred to as secondary store.

bar code Information displayed as black and white stripes which represent a digital code. The black and white lines represent 1s and 0s and can be read by an optical reader.

Most bar codes on products have thirteen numbers, the first two normally show which country the product comes from; for Britain that number would be 50. The next five figures represent the company or factory that made the goods, while the next five figures show exactly what the item is, eg a bar of chocolate, a tin of beans. The last number in the bar code is a check digit and is there to check that the computer has read the other figures correctly. Certain products only have eight numbers in their bar codes. Some television video recorders use bar codes to set timing mechanisms for recording programmes. (See **Figure 4** on page 50.)

bar-code reader An optical reader used to scan and input information represented by bar codes.

BASIC An acronym for **B**eginner's **A**ll-purpose **S**ymbolic **I**nstruction **C**ode. A high-level computer language designed for easy use. BASIC is the language supplied with most home microcomputers.

batch processing As a term used in data processing. The running of a set of jobs, each of which processes a collection or batch of data. An example would be a payroll run where all the data prepared for a particular run would be input at the same time and then the processing would take place. While the file was being worked on, it would not be available for use by other users. (Compare and contrast with **real time**.)

baud A unit for measuring the speed at which information is transmitted per second, eg in the binary system a baud rate of

1200 means that 1200 bits will be transferred every second. The higher the baud rate the faster your computer system can receive or send information.

binary A numbering system based on the number 2. The only digits needed to express any number are 0 and 1, eg 1001 = 9. The binary number system is important as it is the means by which instructions are understood by computer system. (Compare and contrast with **decimal** and **hexadecimal systems**.)

bit **BI**nary digi**T**. This is the smallest unit of information. It is the on/off pulse of computer code. In binary code this is represented as either 1 or 0. Eight bits make a byte. (See also **byte**, **kilobyte** and **megabyte**.)

block As a term used in word processing and text editing. It is an identified section of text. Once the section of text has been identified, it is then usually possible to cut/delete, move or copy the section. The block may be identified by highlighting or by putting markers at the start and end of the section.

board A flat base or board on which other electronic devices such as chips are mounted. (See also **printed circuit boards** and **motherboards**.)

bootstrap An electrical signal triggered by a key depression or when a computer is switched on. The signal causes a short program to load the main program from a particular device.

buffer An area of memory that is used as a temporary store for instructions or data being transmitted from one part of a computer system to another. The buffer receives the information from the sending device and stores it until the receiving equipment is ready to process the information. Printers often have a buffer memory.

bug A term used to describe a mistake or problem in a computer program. It could also refer to a hardware fault.

bulletin board A facility offered by computer networks which allows messages to be placed in a particular location which can be accessed by all users of the network. An electronic version of a noticeboard.

bus A pathway consisting of one or more wires that connect two or more devices. For example, a data bus will be the wires that connect the devices that can send and receive data. (See also bus as a form of network organisation under **networks**.)

byte A unit that is used to measure or express the quantity of data or memory capacity of a computer. Most computer systems use one byte, which is equivalent to eight bits, to represent an item of information such as a letter, number or other character. There are 256 different combinations made by rearranging the 0 and 1 bits in an 8-bit byte. (See also **bit**, **kilobyte** and **megabyte**.)

C

CAD	computer aided design
CAL	computer aided learning
CAM	computer aided manufacture
CD	compact disk
CNC	computer numerical control
COBOL	common business oriented language
CP/M	control program for microcomputers
CPS	characters per second
CPU	central processing unit
CUG	closed user group

CAD Computer Aided Design. The use of a computer system to help in the process of design, eg draughtsman, pattern making. Designs can be saved and recalled and amended as necessary.

CAL Computer Aided Learning. The use of a computer system in education and training to provide learning and teaching materials. There is a wide variety of ways in which the programs can interact with the learner.

CAM Computer Aided Manufacture. The use of a computer system to help manufacture a product. The term can also include automatic stock control, goods ordering systems and robot controlled machines.

cartridge A device that can be plugged into a socket in a computer system. It can be used to hold extra ROM chips.

Ceefax The name of the teletext service provided by the BBC. The service was started in 1976 and it is transmitted on BBC1 and BBC2. It transmits news bulletins, financial and travel information, etc.

cell As a term used in spreadsheet applications. It refers to the box or square on a spreadsheet into which text, numbers or a formula can be entered. (See also **spreadsheet** and **Figure 2** on page 48.)

character A term used for any of the letters, numbers, signs and symbols on a screen or print-out. For example, HELLO OUT THERE! is made up of 16 characters. Each character is represented in the computer by its own individual pattern of binary numbers.

check digit A number or character that is placed after an identifier number. Its purpose is to check that the first and identifying part of the number has been entered into a computer system correctly.

chip As a term used in microelectronics and computing. An integrated circuit, made of silicon, on which thousands of tiny electronic circuits are etched. For protection chips are enclosed in ceramic or plastic cases; these can then be plugged into circuit boards or cartridges.

circuit As a term used in transmission circuit, communications circuit or data circuit. It describes a two-way route joining at least two devices allowing an exchange of signals in either direction.

closed user group (CUG) A particular group of users in a viewdata system. The group of users will be the only one who can access certain information or communicate via that viewdata system, eg travel agents.

CNC Computer **N**umerical **C**ontrol. A method of controlling a machine by numeric input, eg a CNC lathe. A computer is loaded with a program that is used to instruct the machine or lathe to carry out a series of actions. The value of the numeric input will determine the actions carried out.

COBOL A computer language designed for and used extensively in data processing. The name is derived from **CO**mmon **B**usiness **O**riented **L**anguage.

code A set of computer program instructions.

column As a term used in spreadsheet applications. A vertical line of boxes or cells running down the spreadsheet. (See also **spreadsheet** and **Figure 2** on page 48.)

compact disk (CD) A disk of large storage capacity. The information is retrieved by reflecting a laser beam over the recording surface. CDs are used for audio recordings and offer a higher quality of sound than is available from other recording sources.

compiler A program that converts a high-level language into a computer's machine code or other low-level language. The compiler translates the whole program into machine code before the program can be used by the computer. Compilers are more efficient than interpreters but harder to use. (Compare and contrast with **interpreter**.)

computer An electronic, programmable machine that processes data. A computer can follow and carry out instructions given to it in the form of a program. It can store data in its memory; it can perform calculations on data given, move, order and sort data and make some simple decisions. Computers cannot do anything without being given instructions. Every computer consists of the following parts – input device, processor, memory and output device.

computer system A central processor together with its peripheral equipment.

corrupt As applied to data or programs that contain errors.

CP/M Control Program for Microcomputers. An operating system that first became available in 1975. It is available on many different machines.

CPS Characters Per Second. A measure of speed of data transfer, it is often used to measure how fast a printer operates.

CPU Central Processing Unit. The part of the computer to which all the other devices are joined and which controls the overall operation of the system. It is sometimes referred to as the 'brain' of the computer. It consists of a control unit, an arithmetic and logic unit and storage locations.

crash A description of any condition on a computer system that causes processing to fail irretrievably.

cursor An indicator or a marker on a screen or VDU that shows where the next character keyed in will appear. It can be a flashing light, a line or some other indication depending on the program or computer system being used.

D

DBMS	data base management system
DIN	Deutsche Industrie Norm
DOS	disk operating system

daisywheel printer (See **printers**.)

data Information that is worked on by the computer. It can be letters, words, numbers or symbols. A distinction needs to be made between data and information. Data becomes information after it has been put into some meaningful, useful form. Data is put into the computer and hopefully the output will be in the form of information.

data base An organised set of information that is stored in a computer system. The information held can be retrieved, updated and extended. The user, via the software, controls how the information can be sorted and searched and which items can be recalled and how they may be presented.

Key terms associated with data bases are: FILE, RECORD, FIELD.

data base management system (DBMS) A program or collection of programs that allows the user to make use of a data base. It offers the facilities to create the data base, update, retrieve and process data. The use of a DBMS allows retrieval and maintenance of data in a manner that is relatively easy for the user to operate.

data capture A description applied to how the data is collected before it is put into the computer.

data entry A description of how the data was input into the computer system. The main method of data entry is via a keyboard.

data processing All aspects concerning the use of data in connection with a computer system. It refers to collecting, storing, processing and transmitting of information.

data protection A range of activities that safeguard the integrity, privacy and security of data.

Data Protection Act An Act of Parliament that became law in 1984. It is concerned with 'personal data'. The Act gives rights to individuals about whom information is recorded on computers. The Act requires that those, who store information that has been automatically processed and which relates to living individuals, register and record the fact and uphold certain principles concerning accuracy and security of information.

The Data Protection Act 1984 is complicated and it may be helpful to write to the Registrar, the Office of The Data Protection, Springfield House, Water Lane, Wilmslow, Cheshire SK9 5AX to obtain the summary booklets available.

debugging The activity of locating and removing of errors or 'bugs' from a computer program so that the program can perform the task expected of it in order to give correct results.

decimal system A numbering system with a base of 10. It is the numbering system with which you are most familiar. Also known as denary. (Compare and contrast with **binary** and **hexadecimal**.)

dedicated A computer or other device that is assigned or designed for one particular use or application. For example, a dedicated word processor would be a microcomputer designed to offer word processing facilities only.

default value A value or action assumed by a computer unless it is otherwise instructed. For example, if in a word processing program the margins are set at five characters from the left when you switch on the system, then the default value is five. If a different setting is required, then the appropriate command will be needed.

desk-top publishing A description applied to the production of documents using a computer system. It offers more than word processing facilities in that it allows for layout features such as boxes, shading, different fonts for characters and graphics. It is possible to transfer word processed files and pictures created in graphics packages into a desk-top publishing system. The actual facilities offered will depend on the software.

digital information The form of information that can be handled by computers and other microprocessor based technology. The information can be written down as 0s and 1s or sent in coded pulses of electricity or light. The reading is either on or off, or, at one value or another, unlike an analogue reading, which is variable.

digitiser A device that converts data from its given form into digital data.

DIN plug A type of plug that has a number of pins, usually five or seven, and is surrounded by a metal ring. Such a plug can be used for a variety of uses including connecting a cassette recorder to a computer. **D**eutsche **I**ndustrie **N**orm is the German equivalent of the British Standards Institution.

diode A semiconductor component that allows electric current to flow in one direction only.

direct access A system of storing data so that it can be retrieved directly without having to search through any other stored data. This system can also be described as random access.

disk A computer storage device. Disks are coated with a substance that can be magnetised. The disk is divided into tracks and each track is divided into sectors. There are several types of disks; they may be used to store information and allow information to be taken from store, ie read from, or allow information to be saved, ie written to.

The two main types of disks are floppy or hard disks. The most common sizes of floppy disks currently in use are 5¼ inch, 3½ inch and 3 inch. Disks can be double sided, ie both sides of the disk can be used for storage, or single sided where only one side of the disk is used for data storage. Disks can also be described as double density or single density. Double density disks store twice as much data as the single density disk of the same size. (See **Figure 3** on page 49.)

disk drive A device that allows information to be read from, or written to, magnetic disks. The device has a read/write head and rotates the disk in order to gain access to the whole of its surface.

disk operating system (DOS) A utility program that will manage the programs and data files stored on a disk.

Domesday project An interactive video disk program that contains national information including maps, statistics and pictures of different parts of the UK.

dot matrix printer (See **printers**.)

download The act of receiving a program sent along telephone wires or through a communication system. The term can also be used to describe the transfer of programs or data from a mainframe computer to other computers. The reverse process would be known as upload.

dump An operation in which the contents of a computer's memory are transferred to another part of the memory or an output device such as a screen or printer.

E

EFT	electronic fund transfer
EFT/POS	electronic fund transfer at point of sale
EMail	Electronic mail
EOL	end of line

Econet The trade name given to a local area network for the BBC computer.

edit A description of the activity of changing or correcting text or other entries on a computer system. It is often used with computer application packages such as word processing and spreadsheets but it can also be used when changing existing lines of a computer program.

EFT Electronic **F**und **T**ransfer. The transfer of money from one bank or money account to another using electronic and telecommunication means.

EFT/POS Electronic **F**und **T**ransfer at **P**oint **o**f **S**ale. The electronic transfer of money from a customer's account to the retailer's account at the time of purchase of an item. The transaction is made possible by use of a 'plastic card' which is encoded with details of the customer's account, bank, etc.

electronic mail (Email) A method of communication using computer systems or other electronic means. The user keys in a message on the system and sends it to another user via the computer network. Electronic mail software packages often provide the means to send, view, print, save and delete messages.

electronics An area of study concerning the behaviour of electrons, that is the control of tiny electric currents. Digital watches, transistor radios, calculators and computers all work by means of electronics.

embedded commands As a term used in word processing or text editing. These are commands given to a word processing system affecting the layout and formatting of the text when it is printed. The screen layout may not change but the instructions will be carried out when the document is printed.

emulator A program that allows the computer to behave or respond as if it were something else. For example, a teletext emulator will allow the computer to act as a teletext system.

end of line (EOL) A key on the keyboard which will allow the cursor to move directly to the end of a line of text.

expert system A computer program that attempts the job of a skilled human expert. Knowledge from many specialists is fed into the computer to form rules. The computer then makes decisions on the basis of these rules.

F

FIFO	first in first out

facsimile transmission FAX machines. A device that can send and receive any kind of document printed or handwritten, painted or photographed. This is achieved by scanning the document, reading the lightness and darkness over the page. The information is converted into electrical signals that are then sent over the telephone system. A machine at the receiver's end converts the electrical signals into an exact copy of the original. In this way it is possible to send drawings and photographs as well as handwritten text.

fatal error A description given to an error from which there is no recovery.

fibre optic cables The latest form of cable used for the transfer of information. The cables are made of fine filaments of glass fibre about the thickness of a human hair. Electronic signals are changed into light signals by a laser and sent along the glass fibre. Such communication cables can carry more information with less distortion than the traditional copper cables.

field As a term used in data base applications. One heading or section of a single record. Each record in a file will contain the same field headings. (See also **data base**.)

FIFO An acronym for **F**irst **I**n **F**irst **O**ut. A description of the order for dealing with information. It simply means the first item of information stored will be the first to be considered. This is also referred to as a queue. (Compare and contrast with **LIFO**.)

file (1) As a term used in data base applications. A set of records, systematically organised in a computer's memory. (See also **data base**.)

file (2) As a term used when referring to a means of storing information on a computer disk or tape. It is a document of information and could relate to data base, word processing, spreadsheet or other sets of information. Such information can only be accessed through a computer program.

firmware A computer program that is held in a permanent form such as a ROM chip.

fixed length record As a term used in data base applications. It is a predetermined length for a record, which cannot be extended. If the data entered is less than the required length, then the storage space remains empty.

flag An indicator or pointer that is used to signal a particular condition. This may be a set of characters, a single character or a single bit within a byte.

floppy disk A form of computer storage medium that is not rigid. A thin plastic disk coated with magnetic material. Floppy disks are available in several sizes 8 inch, 5¼ inch, 3½ inch and 3 inch. (See **Figure 3** on page 49.)

Also known as a diskette. (See also **disk** and compare and contrast with **hard disk**.)

flowchart A method of representing, in diagramatic form, the logical steps and processes that must be taken to solve a problem. There are several standard symbols used. Flowcharts are often used in the early stages of planning a computer program or system.

font A set of printing or display characters in a particular type style. Some word processing and desk-top publishing systems will offer a choice of fonts.

format (1) As a term used in word processing. It refers to changing the layout of text by altering the line spacing and/or margins and displaying the work with justification on or off.

format (2) As a term used in preparing disks for use. Brand new disks need to be formatted before they can be used with a particular computer system. The format will be a magnetic pattern imprinted on a disk. The user will not be able to see where the tracks and sectors have been set up. This process can also be referred to as initialising.

frame A single screen-sized picture of videotex-type information. It is possible to have more than one frame to a page of videotex.

function keys Some computer systems offer such keys on the keyboard. They will allow certain actions to be performed by pressing the appropriate key. It is possible for each program used on the computer system to use the function keys in a different way. To help the user remember which key to press, key strips are often supplied with software. (See **Figure 7** on page 53.)

G

GIGO	garbage in garbage out

gateway A means of allowing two different systems to talk to each other even though they are using different sets of rules on their networks. An example of a gateway would be using a viewdata system such as Prestel or TTNS to gain information from another viewdata system such as NERIS.

generation (1) A means of identifying advances in computer technology. Clearly defining each generation is problematic but in general terms this would be as follows:

first generation Early machines that used electronic valves which were slow, expensive and unreliable.

second generation Machines that used transistors as a basic component.

third generation Machines that used integrated circuits and basic operating systems.

fourth generation Still using integrated circuits but referring to the technology of the mid-eighties offering more power, standard operating systems and relative economy.

fifth generation Future technology. Fast processing with input and output mechanisms that will be based on human voice and touch, creating operational expert systems and faster communications links.

generation (2) A reference to the age of a file. For example, the current generation is the latest copy.

giga byte A unit of measurement of the size of computer memory. It represents approximately 1 000 000 000 bytes of storage, its exact value is 1 073 741 824.

GIGO An acronym for **G**arbage **I**n, **G**arbage **O**ut. A reminder that the information you get out of a computer is only as reliable as that which you put in.

global As used in connection with an application program. For example, if you wish to search and replace every entry of a particular word in a word processing document with an alternative, you would search and replace globally.

graphical representation of data Data produced in the form of a pie chart, bar chart or line graph.

graphics Information or data that is presented in the form of drawings, pictures, diagrams, charts or graphs. Computer graphics is the use of computers to process data to produce graphic displays.

graphics pad or graphics tablet An input device. It is connected to the computer and operated by drawing on a flat board with a special pen. The shapes drawn are sent to the computer as binary data. The computer can store and process this data and it can be used to produce the drawing directly on the VDU or as print-out. This type of input device is used extensively in computer aided design (CAD), fashion design, cartoon animation, etc.

H

hacker A person who illegally accesses a computer network system by using unauthorised passwords.

hacking The process of entering a network computer system illegally.

handshaking The exchange of predetermined signals between two devices in order to allow them to communicate with one another.

hard copy Computer output produced as a permanent readable copy such as printed on paper. (Compare and contrast with **soft copy**.)

hard copy device An output device such as a printer or plotter which can produce hard copy.

hard disk A computer storage device. The disk is made of a rigid plate on which magnetised data is stored. Although serving the same purpose as a floppy disk, the main differences are the increased amounts of data that can be stored and the increased speed at which the data can be accessed. (See also **disk** and compare and contrast with **floppy disk**.)

hardware The machines that make up the computer system. Computer hardware can consist of the central processing unit, input and output devices, main memory and extra memory.

(Compare and contrast with **software**.)

hexadecimal A numbering system that uses 16 as its base. It uses the digits 0 to 9 and the letters A to F, and as a result counts as 0 1 2 3 4 5 6 7 8 9 A B C D E F. (Compare and contrast with **binary** and **decimal**.)

high-level languages A description given to computer programming languages that use a single instruction to represent a whole group of instructions which the central processor actually carries out. (See also **programming language**.)

high resolution A computer screen picture that can show a great deal of detail by using a large number of small, close together pixels. (Compare and contrast with **low resolution**.)

I

IP	information provider
IT	information technology

icon A function or command that is represented on the screen in a graphic form. By moving the cursor or directing the mouse to the icon and then selecting that icon the activity is chosen. (See **Figure 8** on page 54.)

impact printers (See **printers**.)

information The meaning given to data. (See also **data**.)

information processing The organisation, manipulation and distribution of information. It includes data capture, data storage, data processing, data retrieval and the output of information.

information providers (IPs) The suppliers of the information on the Prestel viewdata system.

information technology (IT) This includes the use of three technologies: computing, microelectronics and telecommunications and how these technologies are used to collect, store, process and distribute any form of information by electronic means. Any study of IT should take account of how it is applied to all aspects of life, work and leisure and should include issues concerning the social, moral and political implications of its use.

ink jet printer (See **printers**.)

input Data or programs that are fed into a computer for processing.

input device Any device that allows data to be put into the computing system. The following are all examples of input devices: keyboard, graphics pad, microphone, joystick, mouse, track ball, light pen, video camera, sensor. (See **Figure 9** on page 55.)

instruction A single order or command to a computer to carry out a specific task, eg to add two numbers together. A series of instructions could form a computer program.

integer Any whole number. As a term used to describe the display of numeric information in spreadsheet applications. It is possible to select the display of information to show a whole number display rather than a number with decimal places. For example, 8.9345 would be displayed as 9.

integrated circuit A silicon chip on which all the necessary components such as transistors, resistors and capacitors have been etched in miniature.

intelligent machines Machines controlled by microchips can be described as intelligent machines as they respond to information given. They will be following a set of instructions, called a program, stored in a memory chip.

interactive video A medium of storage of information that can allow users to access different sequences in a video disk or tape. This may be controlled by the user or by a computer program that will select the sequence in response to the information given by the user. As a result the experience for the user is interactive.

interface A device that links two parts of a computer system.

The device is usually made up of leads and electronic circuits and connects two pieces of equipment, eg a computer and a peripheral. Its purpose is to convert computer signals into those that can be understood by a peripheral and vice versa. Interfaces are necessary because peripherals and computers operate at different speeds.

interpreter A computer program that translates another program into a computer's machine code language. The interpreter translates the program one instruction at a time. Each time an instruction is used, it has to be translated again. (Compare and contrast with **compiler**.)

J

JCL	job control language

JCL An acronym for Job Control Language. This is a high-level language used to inform the operating system about a particular job. It will carry details such as the name of the job and the requirements of the computer system such as the devices it will need and any programs it will require.

joystick An input device often used in computer games. This is a lever or stick that can be moved in any direction and can control the moving of symbols on the screen to the left, right, up and down. There is usually a fire or action button to press.

justification As a term used in word processing or text processing and display. If the text is justified, then spaces or words are expanded so that each line of text starts and ends exactly at the right- and left-hand margin. Left justified aligns the text to the left margin, right justified aligns the text to the right margin. (See **Figure 10** on page 56.)

K

K or Kb	kilobyte

key in The activity of using a keyboard or keypad to input data into a computing system.

keyboard An input device comprising a set of keys which, when pressed, cause data to be entered into the computer. The most common keyboard is the Qwerty (the name is derived from the top six letters on the left-hand side of the board). Another type of keyboard is known as a microwriter; there are just six keys and all letters, numbers, symbols are achieved by pressing a combination of these keys.

keyword search A method of finding information from a data base or file by giving the computer a 'key' word or phrase to search for. The entries in the file are in turn compared with the keyword until a match is found.

kilobyte (K, Kb) A commonly used measurement of computer memory size. It is derived from K meaning a kilo or a thousand. Therefore 1K represents one kilobyte of storage, which actually works out to be 1024 bytes. (See also **bit**, **byte** and **megabyte**.)

kimball tag A piece of card with holes that represent a code which can be input into a computer system. (See **Figure 11** on page 56.)

L

LAN	local area network (See **networks**.)
LASER	light amplification by stimulated emission of radiation
LCD	liquid crystal display
LED	light emitting diode
LIFO	last in first out

languages (See **programming languages**.)

laser An acronym for **L**ight **A**mplification by **S**timulated **E**mission of **R**adiation. A device that produces an intense beam of light which unlike ordinary light goes in one direction only and is made up of one colour. The exceptionally bright light produced can be used for a wide variety of applications including cutting and welding strong metals, operating on patients by surgeons, or to produce holograms. Laser beams can also be used to make recordings, play music and video disks and as a method of transmitting signals along fibre optic cables.

laser printer (See **printers**.)

letter quality A description of the quality of output from a printer.

LIFO An acronym for **L**ast **I**n **F**irst **O**ut. A description of the order in which a program deals with information; simply the last item of information stored will be the first to be considered for processing. (Compare and contrast with **FIFO**.)

light emitting diode (LED) An electronic component, a diode that lights up. It is used as an indicator for when certain signals are received or conditions are met.

light pen An input device that is pen-shaped and sensitive to light. The pen allows the user to draw pictures directly on to the computer's screen.

liquid crystal display (LCD) A method of displaying information that consists of millions of liquid crystals floating in a grid. By applying electric fields to a certain area, only selected crystals will appear dark. This is the type of display often used with a digital watch.

listing A complete set of program instructions printed out or displayed on screen.

load The action of bringing a copy of a program or data from a storage device into a computer's main memory. A program can be stored on disk and then has to be loaded into the computer in order to run it.

local area network (LAN) Computer equipment linked by cables. The different machines can share peripherals like printers and VDUs and can share the same stored information in the network's memory. There are several ways in which local area networks can be organised. (See also **networks**.)

location A part of a memory unit containing a particular instruction code or data. Each location has an address to identify it so that its contents can easily be retrieved when required.

log on/log off This refers to the action or routines that allow users to go into or leave a computer system.

logging-on The action of calling up a computer network and giving a password or code so that the user can have access to the system.

LOGO A computer programming language used to draw and control a turtle. LOGO is a powerful language designed for learning and offers a range of creative possibilities. It is often used in education.

low-level language A programming language that is very similar to the machine language of the computer. (See also **programming languages**.)

low resolution A computer screen picture that shows less detail as it uses fewer, larger pixels. (Compare and contrast with **high resolution**.)

M

MICR	magnetic ink character reader
MIPS	millions of instructions per second
MODEM	modulator/demodulator

machine language The binary coded instructions that can be recognised by the central processing unit of a computer without the need for translation.

magnetic tape An inexpensive way of storing data. It consists of a tape covered in a substance that can be magnetised and which allows data to be stored on the tape by varying the patterns of the magnetised area.

mailbox As a term used in viewdata or electronic mail services. A means of allowing users to send messages to one another. The message is sent to a location, a mailbox, and the receiver can view the message when he or she next uses the system.

mail merge As a term used in word processing. A function that enables a user to combine items of information. The most common use of mail merge is combining a standard letter with a list of addresses.

mainframe The central processing unit of a large computer that services many devices and has a very large amount of backing store. Mainframe computers are larger than micro- and minicomputers.

mainstore The memory storage of a computer that can be addressed by the central processing unit directly. It can be referred to as the internal storage or real storage.

megabyte A unit of measurement of computer storage representing about a million bytes. The abbreviation is Mbyte or Mb. (See also **byte** and **kilobyte**.)

memory A term used for storage. Memory capacity is expressed in numbers of K. There can be different types of memory, eg RAM, ROM.

In a computer system the memory consists of rows of chips that can store information as bits.

memory cards Cards approximately the size of credit cards that have a tiny microchip embedded within the plastic. They can be used to store information. Sometimes known as intelligent or smart cards.

menu A list or series of options available for a user to choose from. When selecting from these options, further choices may be offered.

menu-driven software A computer program whereby the user selects the options available from a menu or list. (See **Figure 14** on page 58.)

merge A description given for the combining of two or more files of data into a single ordered file. When the data is combined, if necessary, it will be reordered.

MICR or MCR **M**agnetic **I**nk **C**haracter **R**eader. A device for reading specially prepared letters produced in ink containing iron oxide. The most common use of this type of font is the automatic reading of bank cheques. (See **Figure 13** on page 57.)

microchips These are made from wafer-thin slices of chemicals called semiconductors, the most commonly used of which is 'silicon' hence silicon chip. The electronic circuits are etched into the chip's surface and different circuits will perform different jobs.

microcomputer A small, desk-top computer making use of electronic chips one of which is a microprocessor. A microcomputer is smaller than a minicomputer or a mainframe.

microelectronics The branch of electronics concerned with the design, manufacture and use of complete electronic circuits within one small unit or 'chip'.

microprocessor The chip in a computer system that contains the circuitry to perform calculations and generally to process and control data.

microrobots These are small robots controlled by microcomputers. A turtle is an example of such a robot often used in education.

minicomputer A term used to describe the size of a computer system. It is a computer that is larger than a micro and smaller than a mainframe.

MIPS **Mi**llions of **I**nstructions **P**er **S**econd. A unit of measurement of computer speed.

mode A way of doing things. A description of a method of operating.

modem A device that converts computer data into signals which can travel over telephone lines. The word is short for **mo**dulator/**dem**odulator. The purpose of the modem is to change the digital signals used by computers into analogue signals which can be transmitted along ordinary telephone lines.

motherboard A printed circuit board that holds the main or principal components of a microcomputer system.

mouse An input device. When moving the mouse on a flat surface, the cursor on the screen also moves. To signal an action, a click or double click is required on the mouse button. (See **Figure 9** on page 55.)

MS-DOS The name of a disk-operating system written by Microsoft.

multi-access A computer system that allows more than one user to have apparently simultaneous access to the information stored.

multiprocessing A computer system that has more than one processing unit. This allows the system to carry out more than one task simultaneously and, by doing so, increases its overall efficiency. The processors are normally linked so that one unit is in overall control. (Compare and contrast with **multiprogramming**.)

multiprogramming A computer system that allows more than one program to be executing at the same time. This is achieved by one of several methods of sharing the processing power of the microcomputer or central processing unit. One simple method would be to share out the time of the central processing unit so that if, for example, four programs were running in the microcomputer, each one would get one quarter of a second processing for each second. (Compare and contrast with **multiprocessing**.)

multitasking This describes when two or more computer tasks are carried out in such a way as to overlap. For example, when a computer is executing one program at the same time as it is printing output from another program.

music synthesiser An output device that gives sounds in response to digital signals.

N

NERIS	National Educational Resources Information Services
NLQ	near letter quality

near letter quality (NLQ) A descriptive term for output of a dot matrix printer which produces a high quality of output. The quality of the impression given by the print-out is near that of a daisywheel printer.

NERIS **N**ational **E**ducational **R**esources **I**nformation **S**ervices. An electronic data base for teachers and trainers that provides learning materials and curriculum information. The first operational phase was launched in February 1987. The information is stored on a mainframe computer at the Open University and can be accessed via Prestel or The Times Network System when using the appropriate computer program.

networks A system consisting of a number of interconnected points. A computer network comprises two or more computers connected by communication links.

network, type of

local area network (LAN) A system of computer equipment linked by cables of a short distance. The different machines can share peripherals like printers and plotters and the same stored information in the network's memory. Local area networks can support gateways or links to other computers and networks via external telecommunication links.

The local area network can be organised in several ways. (See **Figure 12** on page 57.)

wide area network A term used for public telephone network and other network developments allowing communication between distant points.

network organisation (See **Figure 16** on page 59.)

bus All stations are connected to a communication link in this type of network.

fully-connected In the fully-connected network every station is connected to every other station. This will ensure that the network can continue to operate even when one of the stations is out of action.

ring In this type of network stations are connected to form a ring, each station is therefore able to communicate with each of the other ones. If a station is out of action, then the network can still operate.

A *token ring* network is a special type of ring network that is used to connect devices. It will only allow one station to have control of the network at any one time.

star In this type of network one station is situated centrally so that all communications go through that computer. A major drawback is that if the central computer breaks down, then the whole network is affected.

node As a term used in data network systems. A point where a piece of equipment such as a computer connects to the communication lines.

non-impact printer (See **printers**.)

non-volatile memory This describes computer memory that is not affected when power is removed. Information, programs or data stored will be available when the computer system is next switched on. (Compare and contrast with **volatile memory**.)

numeric A set of characters made up only of numbers 0 to 9. It will not include any letters of the alphabet.

numeric control The automatic control of machines, particularly machine tools, using a control process of instructions that are in numeric form. (See also **CNC**.)

O

OCR	optical character reader
ORACLE	optical recognition of coded line electronics

OCR **O**ptical **C**haracter **R**eader. A device for reading specially presented characters.

off-line (1) A description given when equipment is not at present connected to a particular source or if the connection is made not ready for immediate use. A printer can be connected and switched on but not be ready for use because it is off-line.

off-line (2) The processing of information that will be carried out some time later.

on-line A description given when a terminal, phone or other equipment is connected directly to a computer and is ready for use.

operating system A program designed to control the running of a computer system. It remains operational all the time the computer is switched on.

operators The people responsible for the day-to-day running of a computer system. They control the run of jobs, change tapes and disks, operate printers, etc.

optical fibre A very thin strand of glass or plastic along which light can pass and which can be used as the means to rapid transmission of data.

ORACLE The Independent Broadcasting Association's teletext service. An acronym for **O**ptical **R**ecognition of **C**oded **L**ine **E**lectronics. (See also **teletext**.)

output The processed data or other information produced by the computer. Output may be in the form of print, punch cards, display on a screen, etc.

output devices These are devices that allow the computing system to output the results of processing. Output devices include: VDU or monitor, printers, loudspeakers, motors or switches. (See **Figure 9** on page 55.)

overwriting This describes the replacing of information or data with new information. The term can be used in word processing or text editing or in connection with storing of files.

P

PCB	printed circuit board
PIN	personal identification number
POS	point of sale

package An item or collection of software that is designed to achieve a particular purpose or perform a specific task, eg a word processing package.

packet switching This describes the system of sending messages as small, digital packets that can travel through a telecommunications system independently of each other and are then reassembled at the receiving end.

page As a term used in viewdata/videotex systems. It refers to a unit of information stored on the videotex system. Usually a page is one frame or screenful but it can be more, ie a page can be made up of several frames.

page break An instruction or code to a text processing system to begin a new page.

pagination As a term used in word processing and desk-top publishing. A description given to the dividing of text into pages.

parallel processing Computers with several processors, even thousands, working at once to solve a problem.

parallel signals A group of signals representing one piece of information that are transmitted side by side along separate wires. (Compare and contrast with **serial signals**.) (See **Figure 17** on page 60.)

password A word that is used to prevent unauthorised people using a computer system or accessing certain information. Passwords are used for security reasons. A user of a network may be asked to key in a password before logging on to a system.

peripherals Input, memory or output devices that can be temporarily connected to the central processing unit.

PIN number **P**ersonal **I**dentification **N**umber. A number given to the user of an on-line computer system. The number will need to be unique so that when the user contacts the system, the information retrieved or instructions given will relate to the information stored for that person or that particular activity. PIN numbers can be used with other personal identification devices such as cash point cards.

piracy A term used to describe the illegal copying of software. Hence a software pirate is a person who uses software illegally.

pixel A word derived from picture cell (or picture elements). The screen is divided into a grid of pixels, the greater the number of pixels the better the clarity of the picture produced. The computer uses the grid to divide the screen and each column and row has a number. A graphics program will instruct the computer which pixels to light up by giving their row and column number. (See **Figure 18** on page 61.)

plotter An output device. A pen is used to produce graphs, drawings, maps or plans by moving across a piece of paper.

port The socket or point on a computer at which interface or peripherals such as printers can be connected.

POS Abbreviation of **P**oint **O**f **S**ale. An input device that records data of a sale, eg a till at a supermarket check-out. The data recorded could include the price, description of goods sold, total amount spent, time of sale.

Prestel Britain's first public viewdata system developed in 1978 by the British Post Office now known as British Telecom. It provides a vast data base of information as well as a number of two-way facilities such as home banking, holiday and travel booking and mailbox. The information can be put on the system by Information Providers (IPs).

printed circuit board (PCB) A board that was produced to reduce the problems of wiring circuits. At the outset the board is completely covered by copper which is then etched off except where needed to form interconnections. Components are fitted on to the board. Such boards are cheap and easy to mass produce.

printers An output device that produces characters or symbols on paper.

There is a wide variety of printers available such as: Laser, daisywheel, inkjet, thermal, dot matrix.

printers, types of

daisywheel printer A printer that uses a daisywheel to form the characters on paper. The term daisywheel is used to describe a circular spoked wheel, the characters are placed, like petals, at the end of the spokes. The daisywheel can be exchanged if different fonts are required.

dot matrix printer A printer that produces characters made up of a series of dots. The greater the number of dots the better the clarity of the print.

inkjet printer A printer that produces characters by spraying a fine jet of quick-drying ink on to the paper.

laser printer A printer that uses a laser beam to form characters on the paper. It is a fast quiet non-impact printer; the result is very high quality but it is a relatively expensive form of printing.

thermal printer A printer that uses heat-sensitive paper. The characters appear after heated wires react with the heat-sensitive paper.

printers, categories of

impact printers An impact printer is one whereby the print on the paper is achieved by pressing through an inked ribbon. A daisywheel printer is an example of an impact printer.

non-impact printers A non-impact printer is one whereby the print is *not* the result of a mechanical impact, eg a laser printer or a photographic printer.

serial printers A serial printer is connected to the computer by a simple cable and each character sent to the printer for printing is sent along the cable, one bit at a time.

parallel printers A parallel printer is connected by a ribbon cable with many wires; each character is sent in parallel.

printer, operation of a

friction feed The mechanism for advancing the paper by gripping it between rollers is called friction feed.

tractor feed This is the mechanism for advancing paper which has perforations at both edges via a spoked wheel.

continuous stationery The paper is folded into a pile that can be opened up like a fan. It is perforated at each fold to enable it to be torn as necessary. On the left and right sides of the paper are strips punched with holes for use with the tractor feed mechanism on the printer.

individual sheet The paper is without folds or the holes for use with tractor feed mechanism. Each sheet of paper used will need to be loaded into the printer separately.

printers, comparison of

Comparison needs to be made in terms of:
- Cost
- Level of production
- Speed of operation
- Compatibility with software and hardware.

print-out Paper on which is printed material provided from a computer system.

print-out quality The quality of the printed material. It can be described as:
- Draft – a print quality for testing or drafting material.
- NLQ (Near Letter Quality) – a print quality that is above

draft and is almost as good as that produced by a daisywheel or laser printer.
- LQ (Letter Quality) – a good quality of print.

print-out, speed of

Speed of printers can be measured by:
- CPS Characters Per Second
- LPS Lines Per Second.

private viewdata A viewdata/videotex system that is only available to those for whom it was created, eg an information system set up by a single school or college.

program A sequence of instructions designed to allow a computer to solve a particular problem or undertake a particular task when the data required is given. Programs are written in special languages.

programming language The language that computers understand. It describes the set of rules, keywords and characters that will allow users to communicate with a computer system.

Programming languages can be categorised as: High-level or low-level language.

High-level languages
High-level programming languages include:
- ADA
- ALGOL
- BASIC
- C
- COBOL
- FORTH
- FORTRAN
- LISP
- LOGO
- PASCAL
- PROLOG

These have to be translated into a format that the computer can understand. This is achieved by a compiler or interpreter. The resulting translation is in machine code.

Low-level languages
Low-level languages fall into two groups:
- Assembly languages
- Machine code

These need to be translated to machine code.

programmer A person who writes programs and tests that they work.

prompt A sign or message of some sort shown on the screen that lets the user know that the computer is ready for an instruction.

protocol An agreed set of procedures or rules that will control the format of information or data being transferred.

punchcard A medium for holding information. A card in which holes are made; the information is scanned and interpreted by a punchcard reader which is attached to the computer.

Q

QWERTY This refers to the traditional layout of a computer or typewriter keyboard. The name is derived from the top row of letters.

R

RAM	random access memory
RGB	red, green, blue
ROM	read only memory

RAM **R**andom **A**ccess **M**emory. The part of a computer's memory that can store information. It is a temporary or volatile memory and as a result the contents are lost when the computer is switched off. If you wish to save the data or progam held in RAM, you will need to save them in the backing store and recall them when required. Also known as read/write memory.

random access This offers the ability to locate directly the part of the storage you require without the need to search sequentially through the information from the beginning.

range As a term used in a spreadsheet application. The option that allows you to select how much of a spreadsheet you want to print, calculate, save or perform other actions on.

range check A data validation technique that allows you to check that the data entered is within a permitted range. For example, the number given to a month must be within the range 1 to 12, if you gave 15, then the computer would not accept the information and require a new input.

raw data Data or information that has not yet been processed.

read To retrieve information from a computer system.

read only When access to data is such that it can only be retrieved as stored and not modified in any way or deleted.

real time When a system is operating in real time, the results of any updating will have an immediate effect on the data stored and will change it before the next operation can be performed. (Compare and contrast with **batch processing**.)

record (1) A unit of related data, eg an employee record that could contain the name, address, age and current salary of an employee.

record (2) As a term used in data base applications. A complete set of information on one item within a database. (See also **data base**.)

replicate As a term used in spreadsheet applications. A function that allows an entry in a spreadsheet to be repeated without the need for it to be keyed in again.

resolution The clarity of an image produced on a screen. The quality of the image is dependent on the number and closeness of points used to make up the image. If the system offers low resolution, then curves will be presented like steps; if the system offers high resolution, then the image will be more rounded. (See **Figure 18** on page 61.)

ring network (See **network**.)

RGB **R**ed, **G**reen, **B**lue. The colours generated by the signals used by a computer to make colours on the screen. An RGB monitor can use the direct signals to make a clear picture without the need for any modification. This will produce a clearer and sharper picture than that of normal colour TV.

robot There are many meanings to this term but generally a robot could be described as an automatic machine that can be programmed to carry out a job. The word originated from the Czech word meaning 'work' and was first used by Karel Capek in 1921 when he wrote a play about mechanical workers who rebelled against their human rulers. Some robots have become quite familiar such as R2D2 from Star Wars. Others carry out dull repetitive jobs like putting cars together.

ROM An acronym for **R**ead **O**nly **M**emory. The contents of this part of a computer's memory cannot be altered. This is the part of the memory that is used to hold information or programs that are often needed by the machine or user. The ROM usually includes the operating system. This memory is permanent and will not be lost when the computer is switched off.

row As a term used in spreadsheet application. A horizontal line of boxes or cells running across the spreadsheet. (See also **spreadsheet**.)

run (1) To carry out or start a computer program.

run (2) A complete unit of work, eg a wages' run.

S

SPOOL	simultaneous peripheral operation on-line

satellite An important part of the international communications system. The satellite picks up signals with aerials from a station on earth and then transmits them back to a receiver at a different location on earth. Satellite signals from space cannot be picked up by ordinary receivers, special dish-shaped aerials are needed. (See **Figure 6(a)** and **(b)** on page 52.)

satellite dish A special aerial required to receive satellite transmissions.

scrolling The movement of text or graphics off the screen either to the top, bottom, left or right. This occurs because of the size limitations of the screen, the remainder of the text is stored in memory and can be brought into view usually by moving the cursor in the appropriate direction.

search An action, usually carried out on a data base, to find a particular piece of information. All records will be examined and only those that match with the information requested will be selected.

search and replace A word processing function that allows a system to find a particular word or phrase and replace it with another.

sector A portion of a magnetic disk. (See **Figure 3** on page 49.)

sensors Types of input devices that come in a variety of forms. They can generate input in one of a number of ways, eg by light, by pressure, by proximity, by temperature.

serial access memory This describes the sequential storing of information, ie items of information are stored one after the other and can only be retrieved by working through the list of items from the start. Also known as sequential access.

serial signals A group of signals representing one piece of information that are transmitted one after the other along a single wire. (Compare and contrast with **parallel signals**.)

session This refers to the time spent by a user logged on to a computer system.

shared logic A set of programmed logic or logic circuitry shared by more than one program or device.

shift key A key on the keyboard which when depressed allows an alternative output to the screen. The shift key normally produces capital letters and other characters such as £ and *.

For example, when 'a' is pressed with the shift key, the result is 'A'.

silicon A natural substance, similar to sand, found in some forms of rock. Silicon is a semi-conductive material and is used to make electronic components for many applications.

smart card A plastic card of similar size to a credit card which contains a microchip. The microchip contains details relating to the card, eg it could contain an account number so that money can be transferred electronically, or details of a patient's medical history.

soft copy Computer output that is screen-based and as such is non-permanent. (Compare and contrast with **hard copy**.)

software The progams that make the computer operate. There are different types of programs such as utility programs, application programs, operating systems and all are included under the umbrella term of software. (Compare and contrast with **hardware**.)

sort As a term used with data base applications. The arrangement of data into a particular order either alphabetic or numeric.

spool (1) A shared area of storage for data before transferring it elsewhere, eg text files before printing.

spool (2) The act of copying a file to another area for printing or editing.

spreadsheet An applications program that allows the processing, manipulation and display of numeric data.

The information is stored in a grid of rows and columns and can be found in the grid by use of a cell reference, eg Row 7 Column B. Entries in each cell can be text, numbers or formula. All entries can be replicated, which avoids unnecessary inputs. The output of the spreadsheet can be displayed in the format chosen by the user.

£ and p, integer (whole number) or with the required number of decimal places. Key terms: ROW, COLUMN, CELL, REPLICATE.

sprite A shape or character that can be programmed to move about the screen as a single unit.

stack A term used to describe an area of storage or a list that operates on the LIFO principle. This means that the last piece of information added to the stack is the first to be retrieved.

storage Computers can store information in the main or internal memory and also on the backing store. The computer's internal memory is limited and fixed in size.

When discussing storage, there are four main areas of comparison: cost, speed, access and capacity.

store (1) The action of placing data on to a storage device.

store (2) A description given to a medium of storage.

string A line of characters. This may be an alpha string, binary string or numeric string. The string may contain nothing in which case it is referred to as a null string, or it may contain one or more elements, eg:

A	is an alpha string
James	is an alpha string
David123	is an alphanumeric string
31148	is a numeric string.

syntax A set of rules as to how a language can be used. It applies to all languages such as English, French as well as computer languages such as in programming COBOL and BASIC and commands used in operating systems.

systems analyst A person who decides what is the most appropriate task for a computer and how it should be set up to perform a particular job.

T

TTNS	The Times Network System

Telecom Gold An electronic mail system. Each user has a unique address, known as a mailbox, to which messages can be sent via a main computer system. The messages are available for viewing the next time the receiver uses the system. The system offers not only a national but international communications network.

telecommunications The sending and receiving of information in the form of electronic signals over a communications channel.

telesoftware This refers to computer programs that are supplied via videotex or teletext system. Signals are sent over the system and can be saved on disk by users on their own computer system.

teletext A non-interactive information system provided by TV companies, eg BBC offers Ceefax and ITV offers Oracle. Information is transmitted so as to use the spare lines on a TV monitor. A specially adapted TV set is required to receive the information. It is a particularly suitable method for presenting small quantities of rapidly changing information which is presented in units called pages. The user can choose the information required by keying in the number of the page.

terminal An input/output device attached to a computer system. Usually it is made up of a keyboard or a keyboard and screen and may also have a printer attached.

Terminals may be 'dumb' and as such are used to input or receive data, or they may be 'intelligent' in which case they can perform the input/output task and have some processing capability such as data verification, storage or editing facilities.

time sharing A system in which a particular device is used for two or more concurrent operations. Thus the device operates momentarily to fulfil one purpose, then another, returns to the first, and so on. This will make more efficient use of the system and to each person using the system, it will seem as if they have the sole use of it.

touch sensitive screen A computer screen that responds to pressure applied by a finger when someone touches it, or by use of a pointer or wand. The user is usually offered choices from a menu and by touching the appropriate part of the screen a selection is made. The system works by electromechanical means.

track A part of a disk. (See **Figure 3** on page 49.)

tractor feed A method of passing paper through a printer using rotating pins which pass through holes at the sides of the paper.

transistor A small electronic component made form a semi-conductive material. Transistors replaced valves and have themselves been largely replaced by the use of integrated circuits.

transmission As a term used in data communication. It refers to the sending of information of any sort from one location to another.

tree structures A method of storing information. It provides a data structure in which information is stored at several levels. The organisation is such that its pictorial representation would look like an upside down tree (or roots). The points at which the data is stored are called nodes and the connections referred to as branches.

Videotex systems usually store information in this type of data structure.

TTNS The Times Network System. An electronic data base available for use in schools. It offers messaging facilities and includes a large career's data base, information relating to University and Polytechnic courses, etc. Some education authorities create their own local data base as well as the national information sources. Keyword searches are available.

turtle A wheeled robot often driven by the LOGO language. (See **Figure 19** on page 62.)

U

UPC	universal product code

UPC Universal Product Code. A standard bar code adopted by most European countries.

update A description applied to the changing of an existing record, set of records, file or data base in such a way as to make the information contained more recent than before. The possible actions include the addition and deletion of information and the editing or modifying of information that already exists.

user defined keys The special keys on a keyboard that can be 'programmed' by users of the system to perform a specific function or to enter one or more commands.

utility program A computer program designed to perform tasks that help with the general operation of a computer system such as the transfer of data from one storage device to another or copying programs. (Compare and contrast with **application programs**.)

V

VDU	visual display unit

validate A check on data to ensure it is correct or is within a sensible range.

variable As a term used in programming, spreadsheets, etc. A named item that can be given any one of a set of values.

VDU Visual Display Unit. An output device that provides a screen on which to display information.

video disk A hard plastic disk on which information is stored and recalled by using a special video play back machine. A laser beam is moved to the appropriate part of the disk, the laser beam bounces off the dents on the disk and the pattern is turned into electronic signals and then into pictures or display on the monitor.

videotex The generic name for screen-based information services; it includes both teletext and viewdata.

viewdata A two-way communication system in which information is displayed in a page format, eg Prestel and TTNS.

virus A term that refers to a fault in a computer program. The virus can be passed from one computer system to another when they interact in any way. The problem may be triggered off by an event or at a particular date or time.

voice recognition A device that allows data input to a computer system by picking up voice signals and converting them into electronic signals. Thus a computer system will react to the voice.

volatile memory If a memory is volatile, its contents will be lost when the power is switched off.

W

WYSIWYG	what you see is what you get

Winchester A particular kind of non-removable hard disk used on microcomputer systems.

windows A form of split screen where different applications can display their information independently. You can view the data at the same time as options are displayed in a 'window'. There can be several windows on the screen at any one time. (See **Figure 21** on page 64.)

word processing The act of using the facilities offered by a word processor.

word processor A computer system or applications program that is designed to make the manipulation of text quick and easy. The system will offer facilities for the storage, formatting, editing, recall and printing of text files. There is a wide range of packages each offering some, all or even more of these facilities.

word wrap As a term used in word processing. A description applied to the automatic movement of text to the next line when the line you are working on is full. It is not necessary to press the return key when text is input unless a new line is needed.

work station A complete work unit that may be situated near the central processor or remote from it. A work station will consist of a keyboard and screen and possibly of a printer.

write The process of recording information. If you write information to a disk, it means you are recording information on to a disk.

write protected disk A disk that cannot have any data or programs added to its contents. Any data already on the disk cannot be overwritten. There are several methods of write protecting disk, eg you may cover the write protect notch on a disk with a strip or the disk may have a write protect tab to press.

WYSIWYG An acronym for What You See Is What You Get. This term is used to compare the layout of information on your screen or monitor with its appearance when it is printed on paper. If the screen layout is the same as that which is printed, then the word processing system is said to be WYSIWYG.

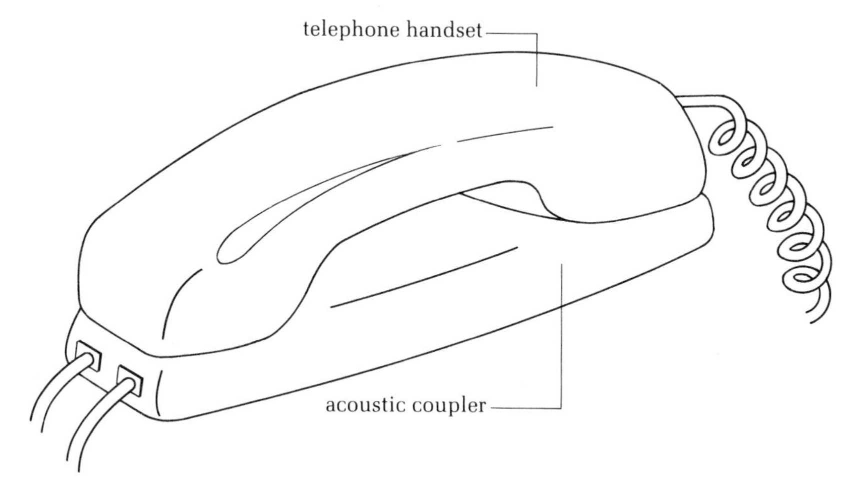

Figure 1 *acoustic coupler*

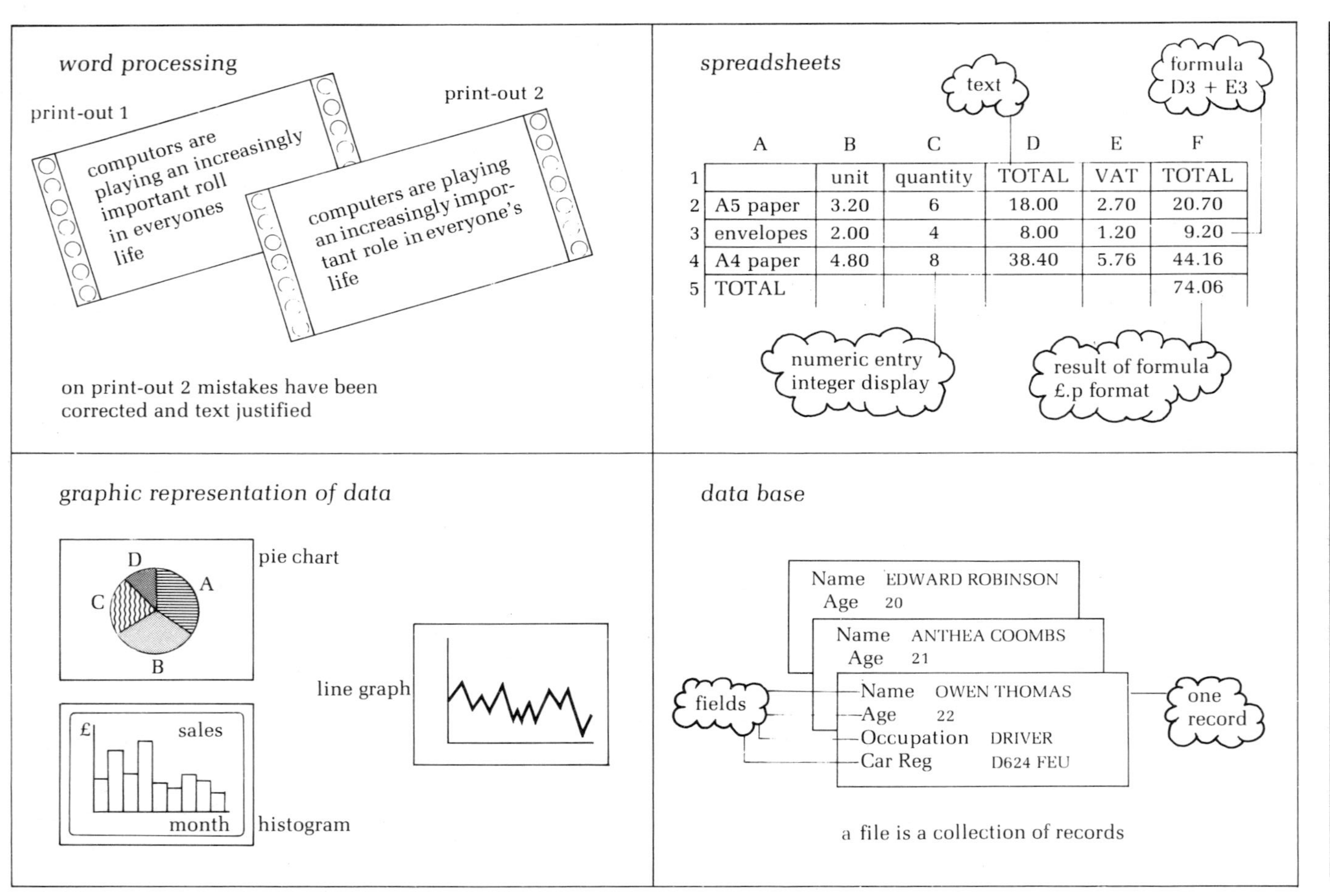

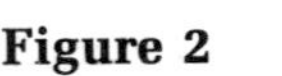

Figure 2 *application programs*

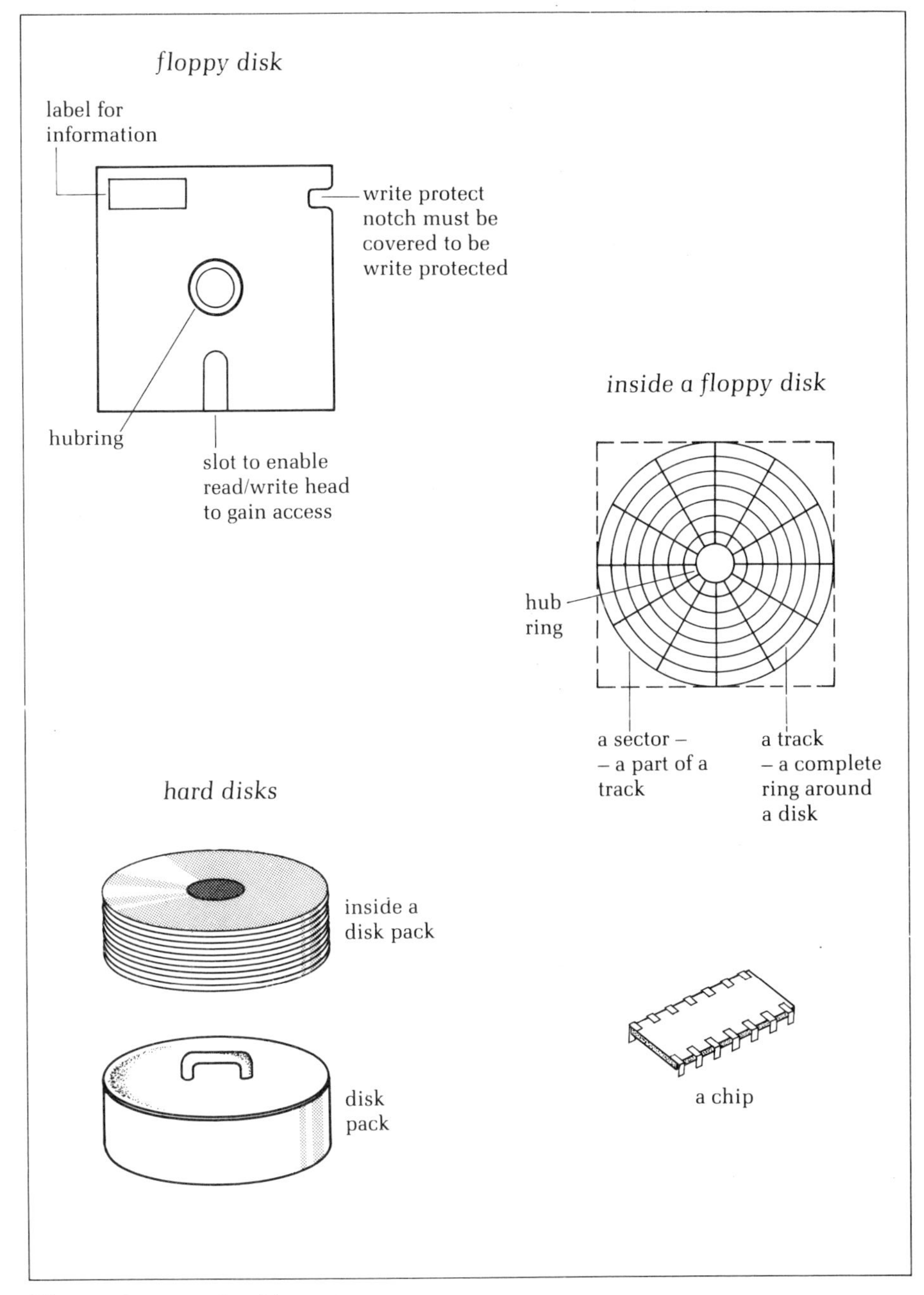

Figure 3 *backing store*

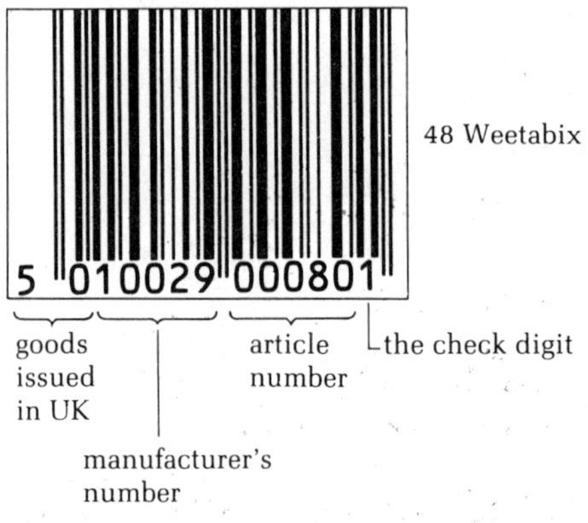

Figure 4 *bar code*

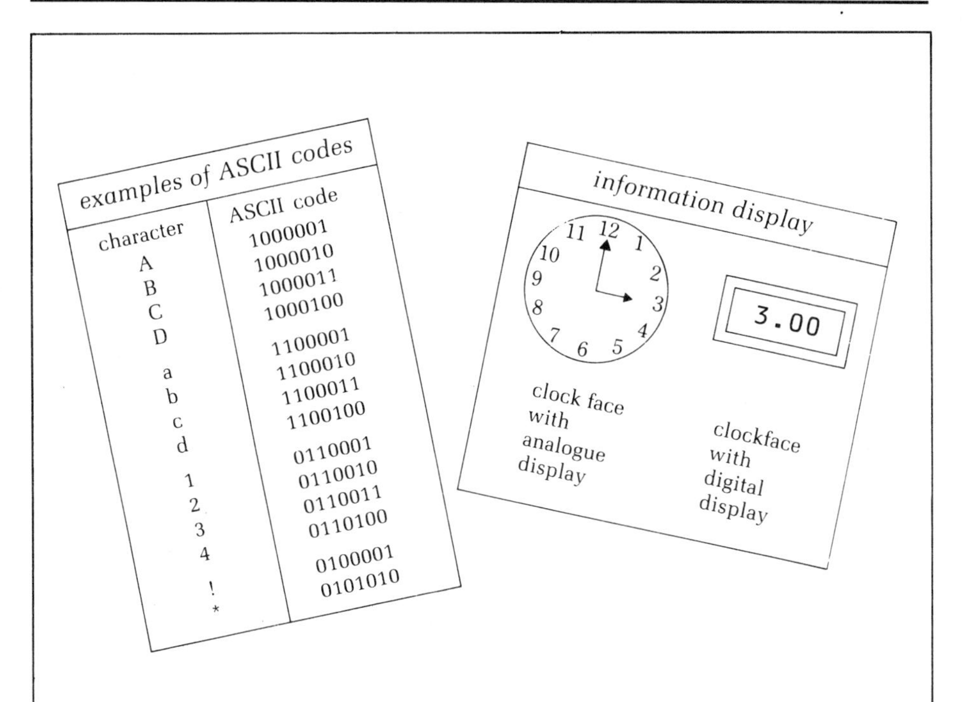

examples of ASCII codes

character	ASCII code
A	1000001
B	1000010
C	1000011
D	1000100
a	1100001
b	1100010
c	1100011
d	1100100
1	0110001
2	0110010
3	0110011
4	0110100
!	0100001
*	0101010

numbering systems		
binary	denary	hexadecimal
base 2	base 10	base 16
0000	0	0
0001	1	1
0010	2	2
0011	3	3
0100	4	4
0101	5	5
0110	6	6
0111	7	7
1000	8	8
1001	9	9
1010	10	A
1011	11	B
1100	12	C
1101	13	D
1110	14	E
1111	15	F

Figure 5 *coding information*

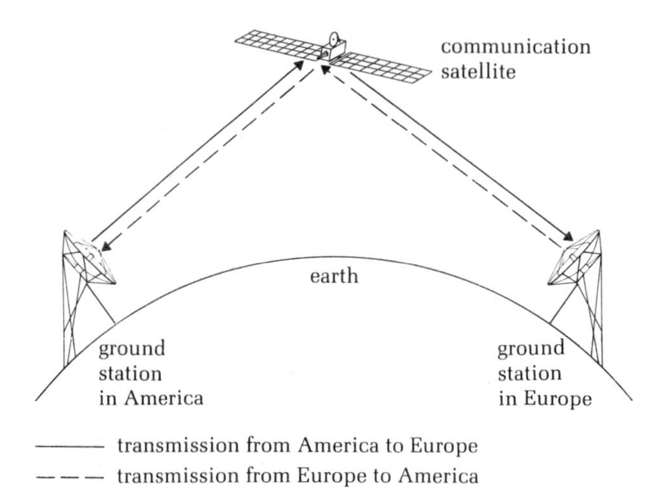

Figure 6(a) *communication satellite*

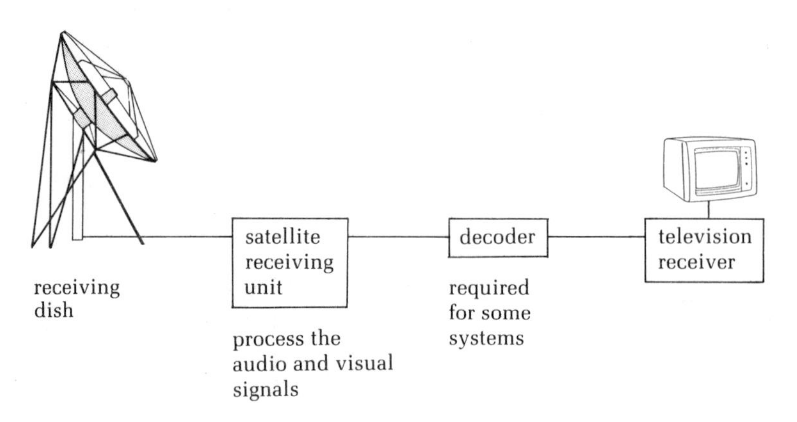

Note: there is a new 12″ flat dish

Figure 6(b) *direct broadcasting by satellite*

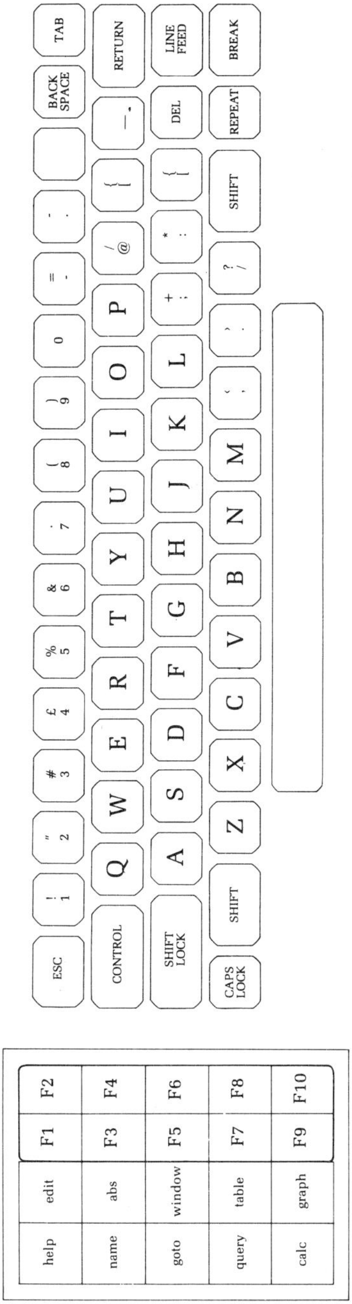

help	edit	F1	F2
name	abs	F3	F4
goto	window	F5	F6
query	table	F7	F8
calc	graph	F9	F10

Figure 7 *function keys*

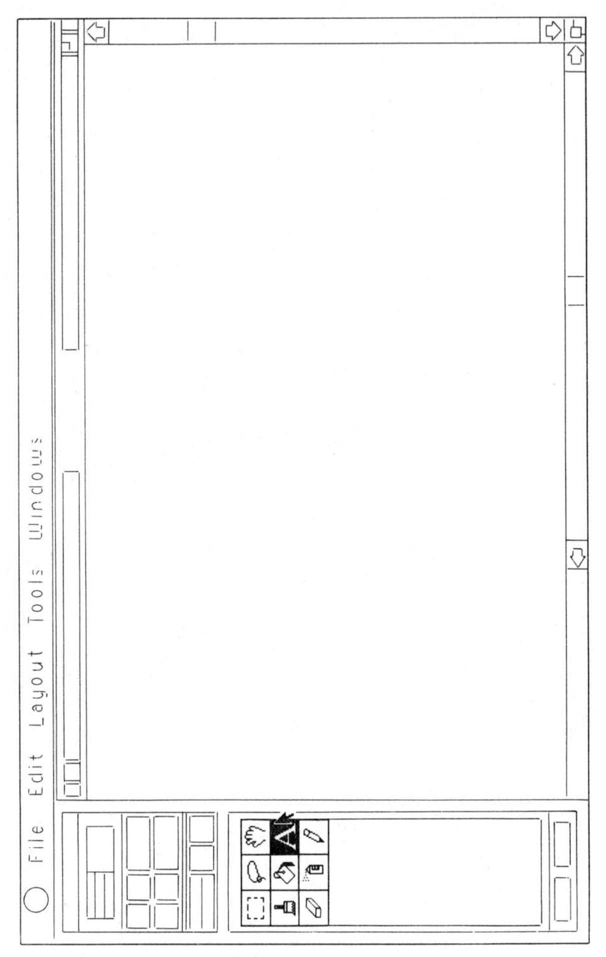

Figure 8 *icon*

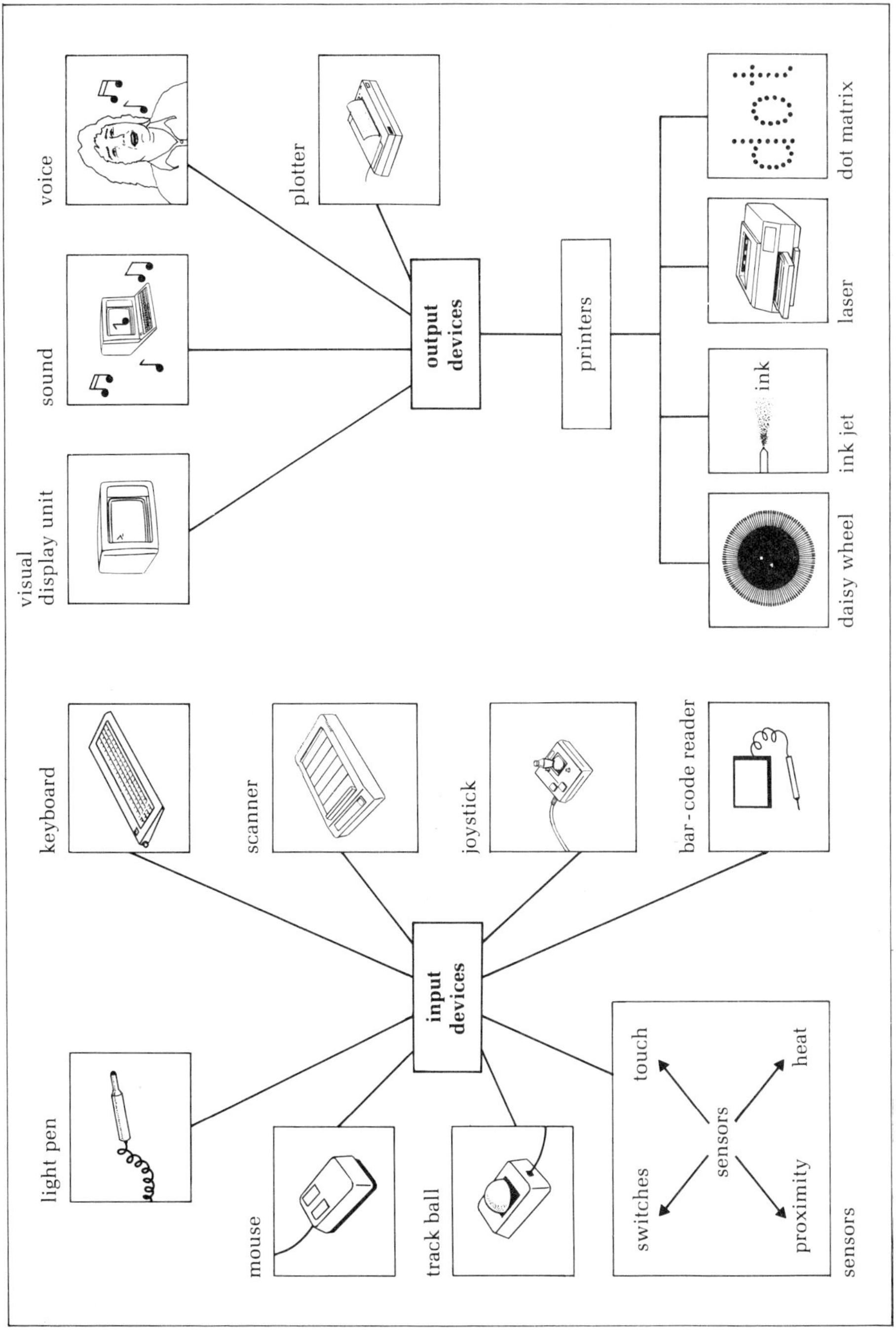

Figure 9 *input and output devices*

```
This text does not
have a justified
right hand margin.
The text has a
ragged right hand
edge.

This   text   does
have   a   justfied
right hand margin.
All   text  extends
to the right hand
margin.
```

Figure 10 *justified and non-justified text*

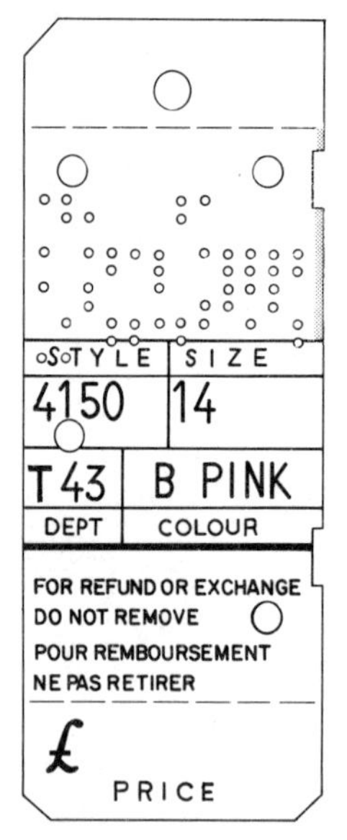

Figure 11 *Kimbal tag*

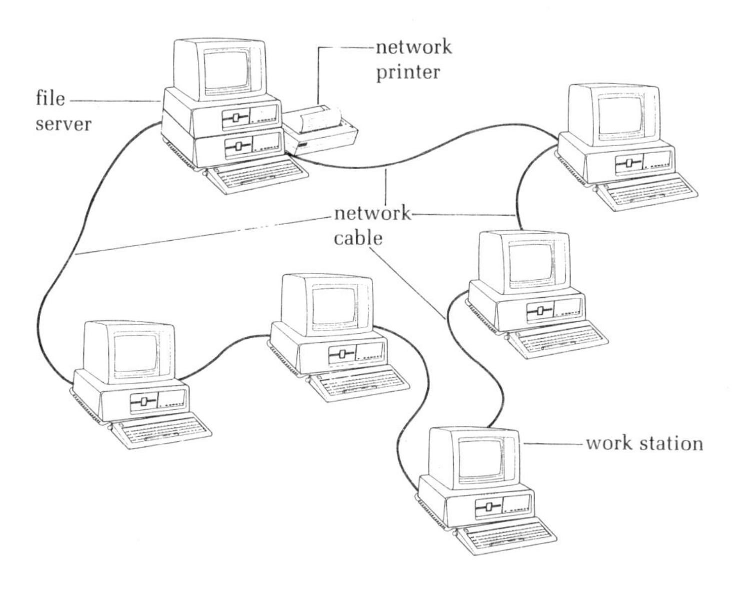

Figure 12 *local area network*

Southern
Bank plc **156 High Street**

______________ 19____ **90-18-40**

Pay ______________________________ or order

______________________________ £

____

____

573059 90 1890 00693912

magnetic
ink characters

Figure 13 *magnetic ink characters*

```
A1:                                                          HELP

Help Index   Select one of these topics for additional Help.
Using The Help Facility              How to Start Over
Errors and Messages                  How to End a 1-2-3 Session
Error Message Index
                                     Moving the Cell Pointer
Special Keys                         Cell Entries
Control Panel                        Erasing Cell Entries
Modes and Indicators
                                     1-2-3 Commands
                                     Command Menus
Formulas
@Functions                           Column Widths
Cell Formats - Number vs. Label
                                     Macros
Operators                            Function Keys
Ranges                               Menus for File, Range, and
Pointing to Ranges                   Graph Names
Reentering Ranges                    File Names
```

Figure 14 *menu-driven software*

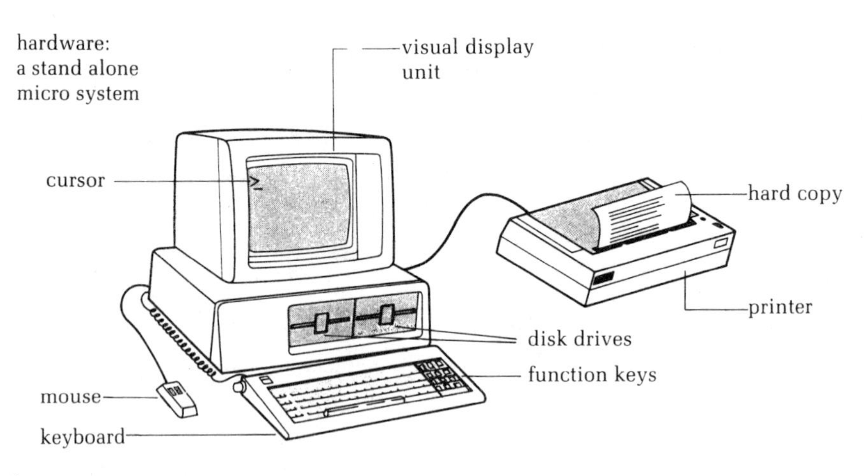

Figure 15 *microcomputing system*

fully-connected network

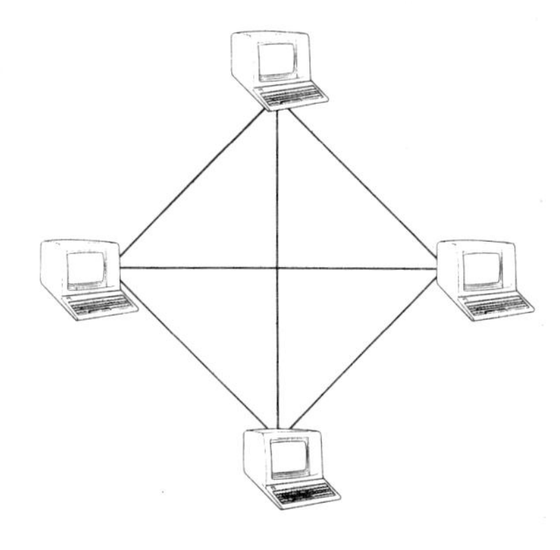

star network

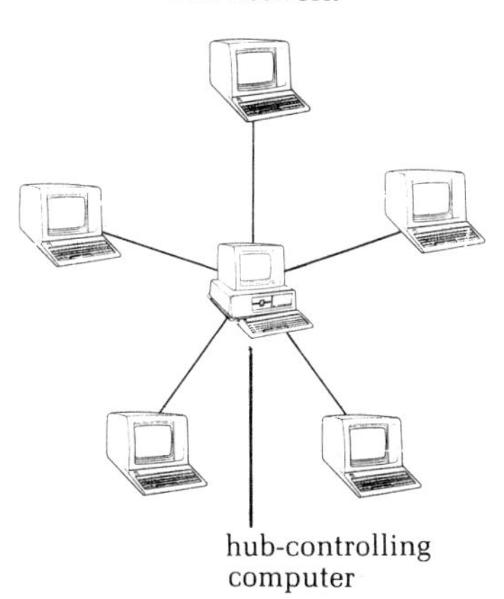

ring network

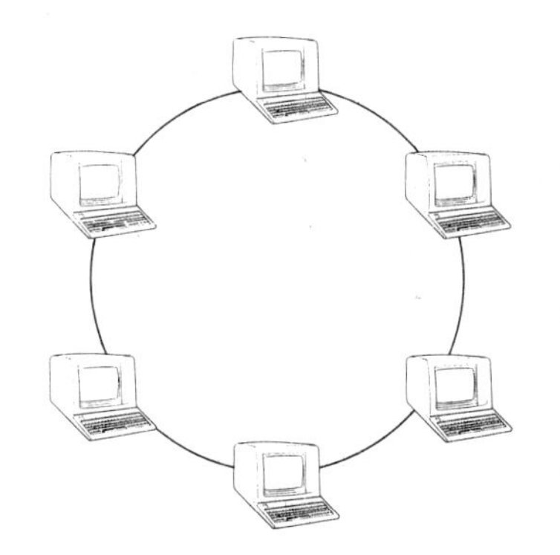

bus network

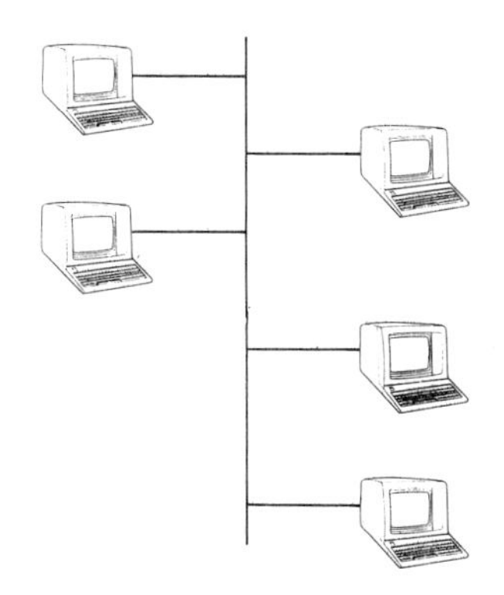

Figure 16 *network layouts*

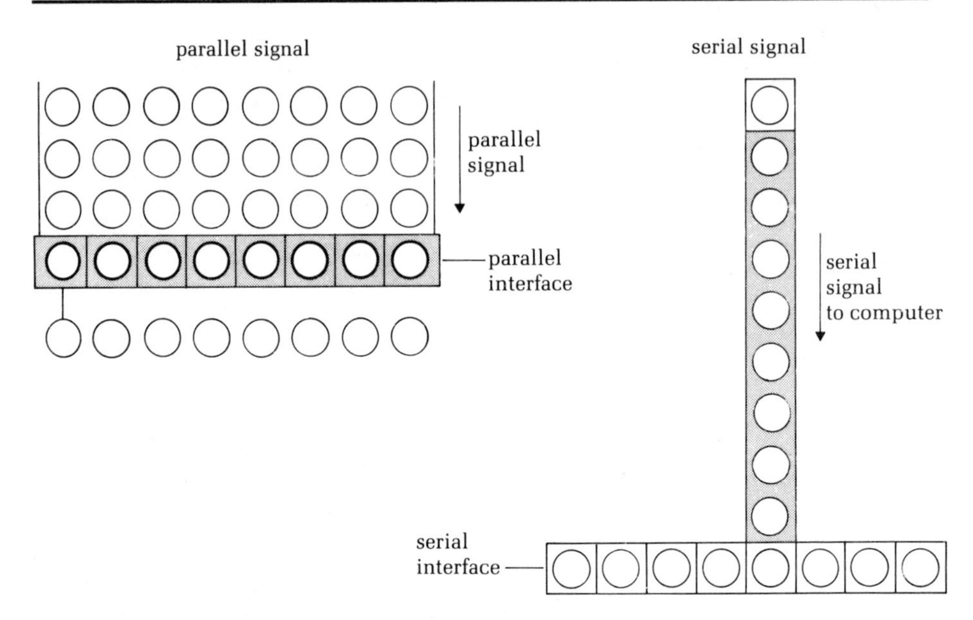

Figure 17 *parallel and serial signals*

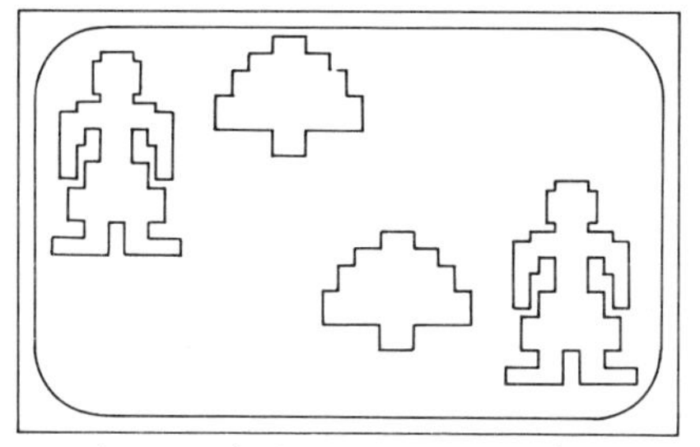

very low resolution (63 × 43 pixels)

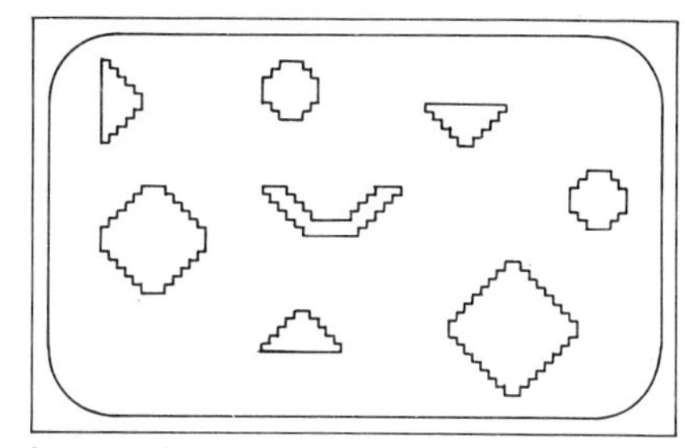

low resolution (160 × 256 pixels)

high resolution (640 × 256 pixels)

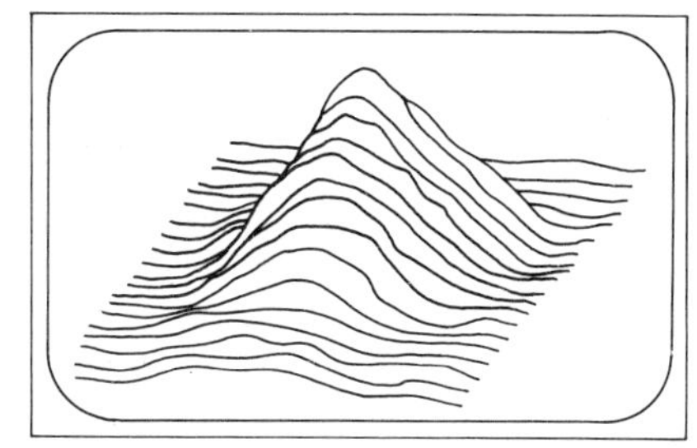

high resolution (640 × 256 pixels)

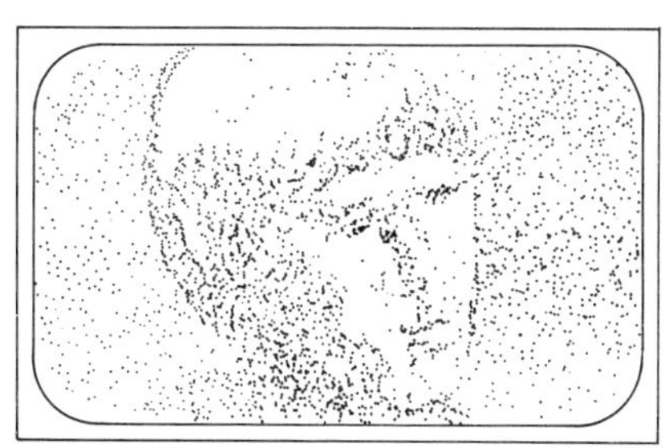

very high resolution (512 × 512 pixels)

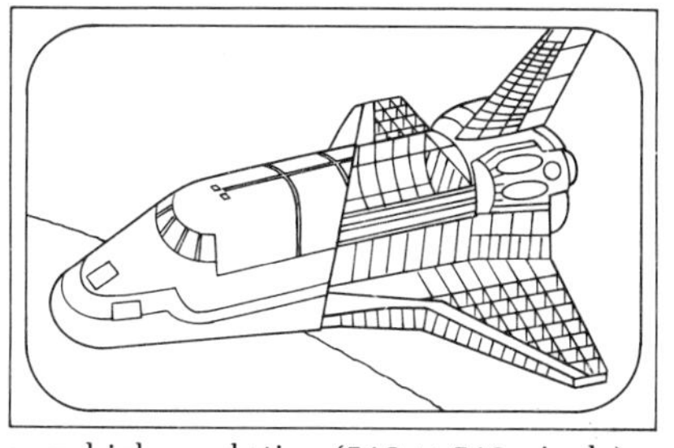

very high resolution (512 × 512 pixels)

Figure 18 *pixel and resolution* The curves in the picture with low resolution are represented like steps. The pixels in the very high resolution displays are almost as small as the dots in the picture of a broadcasting TV programme.

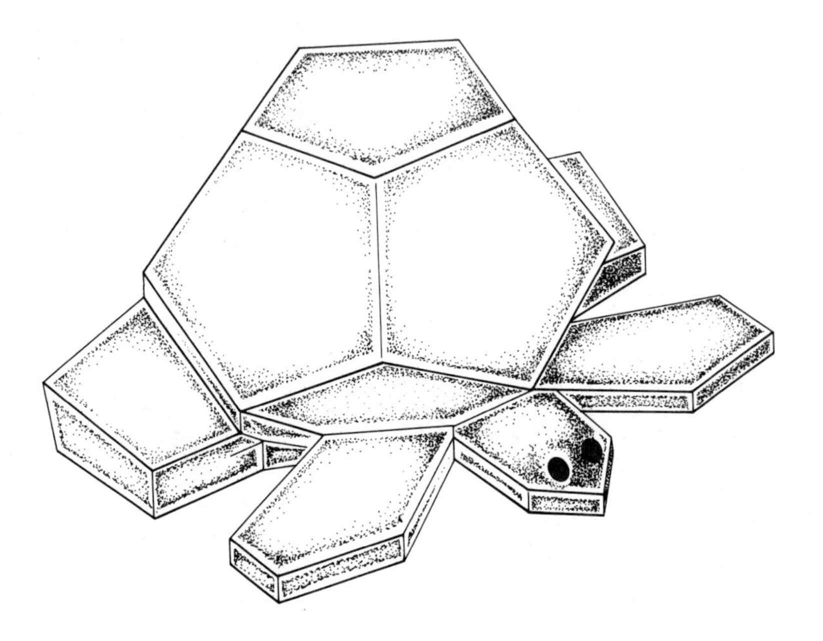

Figure 19 *turtle*

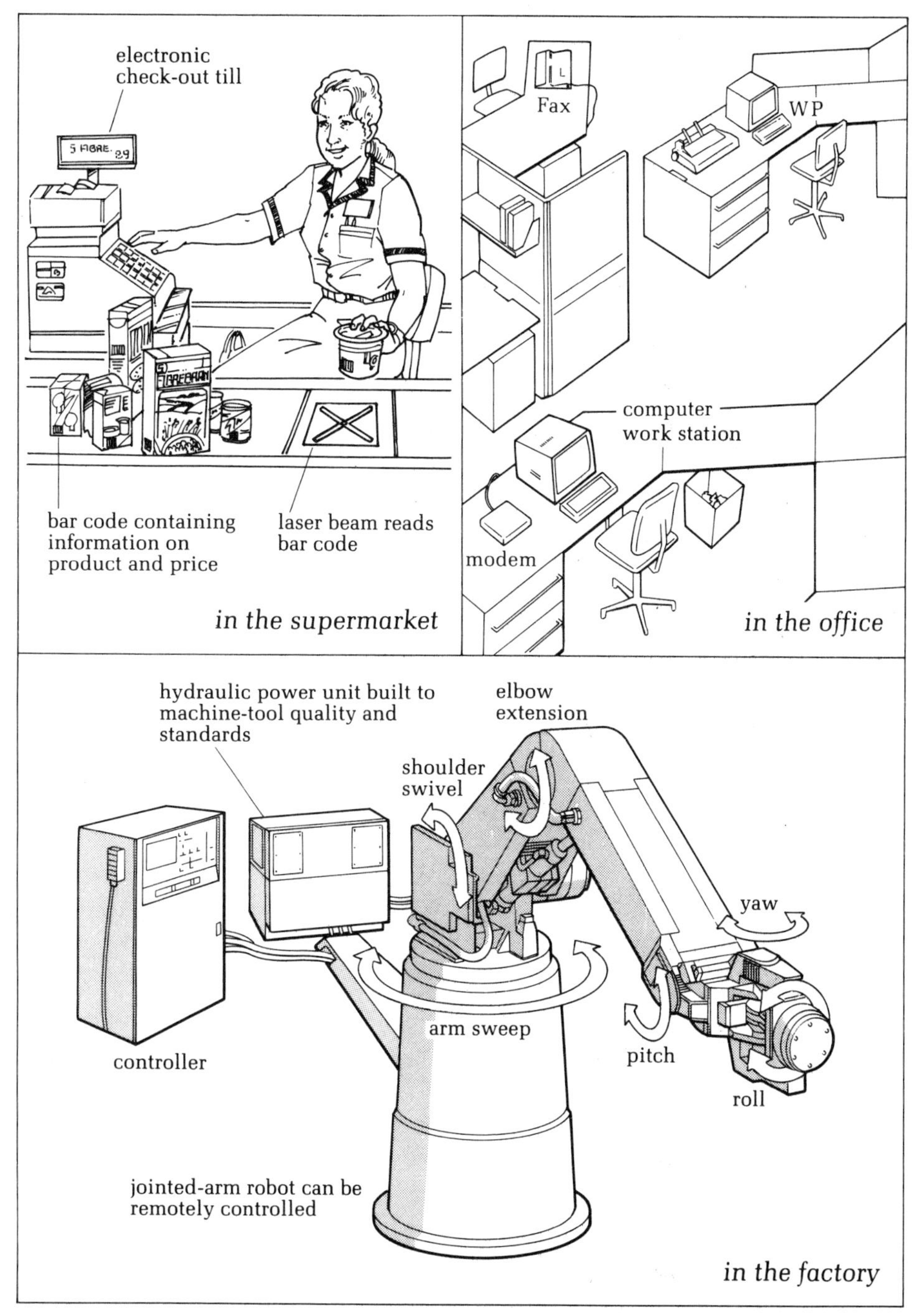

Figure 20 *uses of new technology*

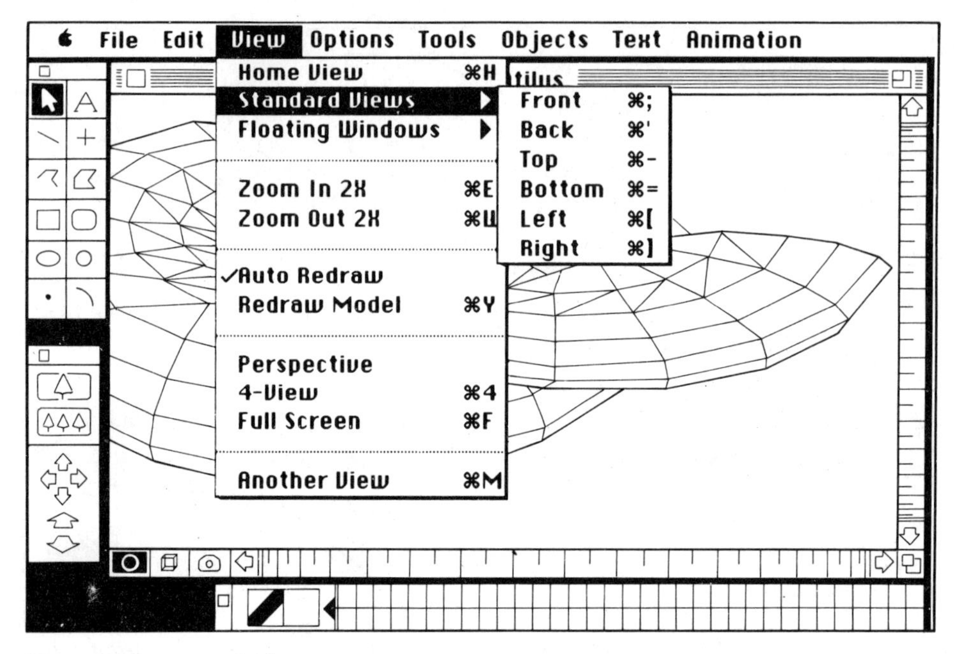

Figure 21 *window*